BE SAFE!!

BE SAFE!!

Little Known Knowledge to Keep You and Your Loved Ones Safe!

Caring Mike

iUniverse

BE SAFE!!
LITTLE KNOWN KNOWLEDGE TO KEEP
YOU AND YOUR LOVED ONES SAFE!

Copyright © 2019 Caring Mike.

All rights reserved. No part of this book may be used or reproduced by any means, graphic, electronic, or mechanical, including photocopying, recording, taping or by any information storage retrieval system without the written permission of the author except in the case of brief quotations embodied in critical articles and reviews.

iUniverse books may be ordered through booksellers or by contacting:

iUniverse
1663 Liberty Drive
Bloomington, IN 47403
www.iuniverse.com
1-800-Authors (1-800-288-4677)

Because of the dynamic nature of the Internet, any web addresses or links contained in this book may have changed since publication and may no longer be valid. The views expressed in this work are solely those of the author and do not necessarily reflect the views of the publisher, and the publisher hereby disclaims any responsibility for them.

Any people depicted in stock imagery provided by Getty Images are models, and such images are being used for illustrative purposes only.
Certain stock imagery © Getty Images.

ISBN: 978-1-5320-6503-3 (sc)
ISBN: 978-1-5320-6502-6 (e)

Library of Congress Control Number: 2018914797

Print information available on the last page.

iUniverse rev. date: 12/26/2018

CONTENTS

Introduction vii

Chapter 1   Freeways, Expressways, Throughways 1
Chapter 2   Mirror Usage 11
Chapter 3   Driving Mistakes 15
Chapter 4   Practice 23
Chapter 5   Avoid Distractions!! 29
Chapter 6   Prepare & Plan Ahead! 33
Chapter 7   Parking Lots 37
Chapter 8   Practice 41

INTRODUCTION

Decisions carry you through life. Some are good; some are poor. We want mostly good decisions. But, it is critical in driving, where good decisions can save your life, and your family, and loved one's lives!

We sometimes use the term "PRO" driver. "PRO'S" are prepared for anything. This takes time and PRACTICE to achieve. It is just a nickname, nothing more, in this book.

On my first full-time job, I was fortunate enough to have a job that entailed driving a car as much as 55,000 miles per year, covering most of the western United States. As you can imagine, I saw some very unusual and dangerous situations unfold over the years. Close to 40 years later, I feel it is time to share some lessons learned, and research I have done. Driving "miles and miles" is over now, but memories are clear.

One day, as I was waiting to enter a major freeway, with no on-ramp, I watched an elderly man pull onto the third lane of the 8 lane freeway, thinking that must be a north-bound lane! Alzheimer's?

He and his passenger were heading the wrong way!! It was a slow time luckily, and he was able to move to the center divider. He continued north for about a mile, until he was able to get off the highway. I could see this unfold, as I went slowly north in the far right lane of the correct part of the freeway. We did not have cell phones then. I did not need to find a phone and call an ambulance or the police.

Today, we have Distracted Driving. We have many other dangers to avoid: Speeding, Drivers "Under the Influence," Texting, and Tailgating. Hopefully this book will point out some remedies for the unexpected challenges you and your families may encounter.

Please read this book many times, and recommended it if you think it will save people's lives.

CHAPTER ONE
Freeways, Expressways, Throughways

CHAPTER ONE

Freeways, Expressways, Throughways

Eventually you will be using freeways to shorten your time on the road, getting to your destination. In order to be safe, and to become a PRO driver, you will need to practice simple maneuvers. These include lane changes, use of mirrors, and turning your head to check out the blind spot(s). Not all situations you encounter will necessitate braking, but at first, most will. First, you must learn to enter a freeway safely and get up to speed as soon as possible. Of course the far right lane goes the slowest usually, with trucks and frightened people going at the speed limit or less. Use of the 3 mirrors is not enough. You must learn to turn your head to the left, quickly, and check out your blind spot. Use your left turn blinker, always, in this situation. (There will be times, in future chapters, when you learn you might not use the blinker immediately.)

This is the time for patience. Busy freeways don't always make it easy to get up to normal speed. The first time you practice, you may want to stay in the far right lane and get off the freeway at the next off-ramp. Subsequent practice runs will take you out onto the freeway for 2 or 3 off-ramps before you get off. Please note that a few ramps do not have the opportunity to turn left at the end and return to the freeway in the opposite direction from which you came. Part of your preparation will have been to get a map of the

Caring Mike

area, or if you are lucky to be driving a car with a navigation system, check the freeway maps and the side streets so you don't get lost. While on these practice runs, get the feel of how wide your car is, by being observant of how much clearance you had when cars pass you. This is a critical skill, and it builds your confidence.

Next

We want to add lane changes to your skills. This one aspect of driving separates the average driver from the PRO's. It can shorten the time you are on the road, and can help you avoid danger, e.g. an unexpected situation that you can avoid by not panicking and by moving out of a lane safely. The PRO's we described in the preface, are those who are prepared for anything. Try to avoid being boxed in at any time, unless you are only moving 5 MPH or are gridlocked. This will give you an escape route! Not many drivers know about this. Be alert for speedsters and those darting in and out of traffic. Also be alert for slow moving vehicles. All can cause a collision or a close encounter. You do not want any of those situations. Slow movers are: texting while driving, frightened drivers and underpowered vehicles like old minivans, some hybrid cars and motorhomes. Trucks are usually slow as traffic builds up, but can occasionally keep up nicely in a steady moving clump of cars. Large furniture moving trucks are surprisingly fast moving, and in the faster lanes. Drivers are still out there with poor vision or skills.

You can find these drivers by being observant, and by using your mirrors (the Six-Steps method.) Habits you form now will keep you and your passengers safe. Nobody wants to be the person who causes a loved-one's injury or death. Habits to forms are:

1. The Safety Check (see Chapter 6)
2. The Mirrors (Six Steps in 1.5 seconds)

3. Lane Changing (Using the head turn)
4. Leave early on a trip.
5. Relax, with No Road Rage (NRR)
6. Become a PRO driver (PRO)
7. Keep a safe distance from the car ahead.

Secrets of the Freeways

Not much was mentioned about off-ramps earlier. Keep in mind that many have signs suggesting a speed that is safe. At first, use that as a guide. As you become more experienced, you will find some exceptions to the suggested speed limit sign. Only use your experience after you are familiar with ramps you know well. Some allow you to turn from more than one lane at the end of the ramp.

In heavy traffic the far right truck lane may give you better headway! Only use this after mastering the lane changes, and using your blinker. Beware a large group of vehicles entering the freeway from an on-ramp. In this case, you should vacate the far right lane and be patient.

Don't be discourteous and hog the number one lane (on the left) or hog the car pool lane (diamond lane.) Some people were given poor advice by caring parents who themselves were worried about lane changes and getting boxed in. Driving too slow in these lanes, if traffic is low to moderate, creates road rage from people behind you, and may create unsafe drivers, who dart in and out of the car pool lane, even illegally. Only if you are a PRO driver with experience, should you test the speed limits of these two lanes.

In heavy traffic, you should welcome the existence of the car pool lane, (if there are two or more people in the car with you.) Not only does it move better than the other lanes, but there is sometimes a safety area to its left, for emergency vehicles, which gives you a safety net if you must bail out to avoid rear ending the car in front who put on their brakes suddenly. Always leave several car lengths distance between you and the vehicle ahead. You can use the old guide of one car length per ten miles per hour, to be safer on the freeways.

During night driving, or while in fog, always turn your headlights on. Do not assume your automatic lights will come on in fog. They will not, unless it is evening. Learn how to work your lights. Do not use high beams in the fog. They will reflect back and blur your vision. Fog is present sometimes during the day. You must help other drivers see you, so use the low beams.

A serious accident ahead of you on a freeway could cause you major delays. Your AM radio may have suggestions for alternate routes, or even side streets. If you are forced to stop, you could check your smart phone for side streets, or check the map you brought in preparation for the trip. Do not do this while on the freeway. Before your trip, use Google Maps or WAZE instead of a paper map, because new technology allows your route to be changed while driving. You are now given verbal instructions base on information about traffic accidents. This can save you substantial time! If you find you are being held down to a certain speed by The Highway Patrol, or State Troopers, you should be thankful they are doing this, because something up ahead is a hazard to you and your safety. Just be patient.

A toll road is worth the money if you value your time. Not only are they newer roads, and the road's surface is smoother, but they are travelled less, and you can make better speeds on these freeways or highways. Warning: they are monitored by police State Law Enforcement.

Beware of tailgaters and drivers who weave within their lane. They may be doing what PRO drivers do not. They may have been drinking or using drugs prior to driving or texting while driving.

Be Safe!!

Learn to use your cruise control on freeways. It can save you gas, especially if you turn it off on hills you are going down. Going up hills, it keeps your speed more steady, but be careful not to get too close to a car ahead. Some cars have a radar attachment to the cruise control that automatically slows you down, for safety, but it does it by lowering your gear ratio on the automatic transmission. This uses more gasoline. On the flat surfaces, cruise control avoids some the accelerator pedal usage that most drivers fall into. Learn how to shut it off to be safe, but a step on the brake will also stop it from creeping up on a car ahead. Never use the cruise control when the pavement is wet or icy. If your car unexpectedly starts to hydroplane, it will accelerate and could take off out of control. Some cars will not allow cruise control when the wipers are on! Most people do not know this danger regarding wet roads.

Until you are a PRO driver, avoid icy roads. Wet roads are a good test of your common sense. Slow down to a manageable speed, and leave more room between you and the car ahead of you. Learn to correct if you start to skid or "fish tale". It is a very easy matter to do the correction once you have practiced it at least six times (three times skidding left and three times skidding right.) This practice can be done at night, when there is light rain, and you have found an empty parking lot with no bumpers at the front of the parking spots. You should locate it well in advance, and be sure there are no stores open there at night. Start your skid by gently turning the wheel to one side while pressing on the brake. Do no panic, just gently turn the wheel to the other side and release the brake. For example, the steering wheel is turned to the left the pressure on the brake. The back wheels will slide to the right. The steering wheel must be turned to the left with pressure on the brake. The back wheels will slide to the right. The steering wheel must be turned to the right (the direction of the skid) to bring the car out of the spin, or to correct for the sliding.

Bring someone with you the first time. Do this exercise more than six times, since you have gone to the trouble to find a great open space in which to practice. It will build your confidence and it will build your driving skills to a point much higher than most of the drivers on the road.

When I was growing up, the high schools would provide "Driver's Ed" courses, usually in the junior year. This is long gone, due to budget cuts. Now you must provide your own driving course with an instructor, if you want it, at your cost. I recommend highly doing this even if you have to give up soft drinks or coffee for a month or two prior to applying for your "Learners Permit." This applies to adults who have postponed learning to drive or those drivers with only basic skills. Just reading this book, will not be enough to mould you into a PRO driver. You must practice, read this book again, and practice some more. Those of you that can afford the course with a professional, but also an advanced driving course with obstacles, spins, and much time behind the wheel, I encourage you to make the investment. My motivation is only to make the roadways safe for you and your family, and for my family too.

MORE SECRETS OF THE FREEWAYS

Once you have managed the mirrors (to be outlined in chapter two), the lane changes, and the other 5-7 items on the list at the beginning of chapter one, you should practice looking ahead quickly, then back to the traffic in front and to the sides using the mirrors. Looking ahead, when you can, is a great way to find your off-ramp, to see traffic slowing ahead for safety, to spot brake lights coming on up ahead, and spotting an opening to enter or exit the car pool lane (as long as you have one or more passengers.) With more experience you will be able to judge the speed of cars ahead relative to your rate of speed. Why? Because cars can slow without the brakes (therefore no brake lights come on.) Going uphill is the most common situation. Keep in mind there are still cars with stick shifts. Car enthusiasts and those that purchase a vehicle with no frills can slow down using the stick shift in a lower gear which increases compression in the engine, which decreases the rate of their speed.

Sometimes you will find an off-ramp that takes you up a small hill to the end of the ramp. Never get too close to the car ahead of you. It may be a stick shift vehicle, and because of the practice of judging speeds of cars around you, you can avoid a rear end collision. (Stick shift cars tend to roll back before accelerating up a hill, even on a slight grade.)

CHAPTER TWO
Mirror Usage

CHAPTER TWO

MIRROR USAGE IS extremely important for safe driving. Why would this be Chapter 2, and not Chapter 4 or 5? The answer is improper turning causes more fatalities than speeding!

Learn to make driving your primary task, not texting, or chatting, or talking on the phone, even if you have Bluetooth. Turns include Changing lanes, U-turns, Left turns, Right turns, and, Exiting and Entering Freeways.

To do these Turns, you need to turn your head to the right and to the left, as well as quick checks of your three mirrors. I know, some of you are unable to glance back over your right or left shoulders, but then maybe you should only drive during low traffic hours! OR, hire an Uber or Lyft driver, OR take a bus or taxi or a ride with friends. I know, this sounds harsh, but this book was meant to help people avoid getting into an accident and killing someone. You would not like your family or friends or their families to experience a traffic death. You would not like your friends and loved ones to grieve over your death.

There are blind spots in your rear view mirrors. The Highway Patrol knows this, as do Police Officers, who I have seen many time over 50 years of driving, monitor a driver, completely out of site, quite near you!

For most of you, please practice making quick checks, one mirror at a time, always back to looking forward before checking the next of three mirrors. Then check both left and right views of the blind spots, separately, by turning your head.

After practicing these moves, then use these skills. First, turn on your turn signal, then check the speed of the traffic. Sometimes it is prudent to start your turn as much as one mile in advance of your goal, if on a freeway with heavy traffic. Then start your 5 checks of cars around you, using head turns first, then the 3 mirrors, then the 2 head turns again.

That's 7 checks!! Practice this and you may someday become a "PRO" Driver. (Not for money, but for your safe life.) Nothing is guaranteed, but sometimes there are nice other drivers who will let you in, to the next lane, when they see your signal on for a while. In some areas of the country, this rarely happens. Look for remedies for this situation in another section of this book, after you have practiced for a few months.

CHAPTER THREE
Driving Mistakes

CHAPTER THREE

DRIVING MISTAKES, including excess speed, are the Number TWO causes of fatalities in the country you live in!

Unsafe speed, not just over the speed limit, causes the MOST INJURY collisions! Chapter 2 emphasized that Improper Turning causes the most FATALITIES.

Injuries can ruin peoples' lives. How would you like to spend months in a hospital? Lose your job? Lose your loved one. Lose your physical ability to work? Lose fingers, an arm, a leg, your sight? Of course not.

I hope I have scared you a little. Now let's lower the odds of that happening!

The 3 Second Rule.

Do Not use this trick just starting out.

Some researchers believe you must keep your car away from the car in front of you, by counting "One one thousand, Two one thousand, Three one thousand", as you pass by a marker on a road, that the leading car has passed before you. This is supposed to keep you safely behind the car in front, whether you are going 10 mph, or 70 mph!

Just starting out, you should not be distracted by trying this trick to keep you safe! After you have driven 50 or more hours, you may be able to pull this off at slow speeds. Experience driving with a parent first, or an experienced driver, or at a driving school. Then you may be able to ascertain a safe distance behind a car, which, of course, depends on the speed you are going. It is distracting to count 3 seconds while picking out a road marker or overpass as a landmark while counting. Don't do this if you are a beginning driver or a driver with little experience!

SPEED LIMITS

Speed limits are set for safety reasons, based on the masses of drivers on the road. The basic speed law states that a person should not drive at a speed greater than is reasonable and prudent for the WEATHER, THE TRAFFIC, THE SURFACE, AND THE WIDTH OF THE ROAD.

This means we could get a ticket for driving below the speed limit in a special situation! You also should not be endangering persons or property while driving.

Fines can range from $100 to $400, depending on the county or township where you are driving. Also be careful about pulling over for an emergency vehicle. Another big fine could be issued to a driver who goes around a school bus with RED lights flashing. Be alert for these situations. When you have done 50 hours or more of driving, and you feel like you want to be a "PRO" driver, you can read my subsequent book or pamphlet on exceptions that can be used safely by yourself and other drivers. This is not "carte blanche" exceptions for "PRO" drivers, just secrets that will help you avoid dangerous situations.

DRIVING MISTAKES

We just talked about speed. Now let's discuss special situations and mistakes drivers routinely make. These may be important for you and your families.

WEATHER. Obvious mistakes are made by many while driving on wet roads, and icy roads. Braking in a panic, can cause your car to slide out of control. Leave more room between you and the car in front of you.

Not all of you have special brakes which can feather the braking automatically (ABS.) Since many drivers have more than one car, some cars may not have that feature, as well as other drivers around you also.

Learn to tap the brake pedal repeatedly until you come to a slower speed or to a stop! Practice, Practice!

FOG. Roads are usually not too wet, but can be, so be prepared: have the headlights on, but never on high beams. You could blind yourself a little, as well as the oncoming motorist. This means fog during the day, as well as the night!

ICE. A very dangerous situation. Postpone driving if you can. If it happens frequently where you live, try to practice during the night in a vacant parking lot, so you can learn how to correct a sliding automobile.

Basically, if you are turning left on ice, the car will slide to the right on the rear tires most times. Correct the slide by turning the steering wheel to the right! Then straighten out the direction forward.

When turning right on ice, and the car slides, it will be to the left! You then compensate by turning the wheel to the left! Then straighten out the direction forward.

After practicing this maneuver a few times, you may be ready to drive on ice if you must. A driving school with expert instructors would be a major help in learning safety on ice. It may take a while to find one, but if you need the skill, please take this seriously. Also, put special tires on your vehicle that have studs to help with ice and snow. Put on your calendar a date each year to change tires when ice and snow seasons start.

WET ROADS. This challenge will be found in most parts of whatever country where you live, at some times of the year. Practice cautionary driving in the rain as soon as possible. Make sure it is not a busy highway at first. Make sure your tires have more than just adequate tread. Many tire dealers will give you a free tire inspection, (in hopes they can sell you some tires.) Take advantage of this before the rainy season, to help you have good traction with the road. Details, details.

See Chapter 6 for maintenance hints to keep you and your friends and family safe.

U.S.A. traffic fatalities rose, starting in 2016, after slowing in preceding years, according to NHTSA (National Highway Traffic Safety Administration.) In one year, drivers travelled 2.2% more, but fatalities rose 5.5%! Motorcycle, and pedestrian deaths rose 5.1% and 9.0% respectively.

Distracted driving is increasing, due to inattention and distractions. Consider Bluetooth for phone calls, so you need not touch your cell phone. Put your phone out of reach while driving, (reaching for it is a major distraction, taking your eyes off the road,) or hand it to a trusted companion in the car when you start your drive.

CHAPTER FOUR
Practice

CHAPTER FOUR

Practice! Practice! Learn evasive driving skills. Driving is not just going straight ahead. You must occasionally avoid drivers who look like they are drunk or stoned on drugs. Weaving is a signal! Excess speed is a signal! Others to avoid are tailgaters (following too close to others as well as behind you.) Plan your evasive tactic before you make any sudden move. Continue to watch the road ahead, behind, and to your two sides. When you can, choose to slow down and look for an opening to move away from the culprit; or, choose to change lanes to move away from the culprit; or choose to wait for another lane to be available. Signal first before changing lanes. Practice! Practice!

Find someone who can help you with evasive skills. In your area, the extra cost may be worth it! There are skills to be learned if you wish to enter freeways safely. On-ramps need your head turning skill to make it safer. Plus, you need to accelerate carefully so you can merge into traffic. Too many beginners panic about getting into position on the freeway. Practice Practice your basic skills on city roads before you begin to enter freeways. Become a great lane changer first.

Off-ramps are substantially easier, if you can change lanes well.

There are online companies available to help drivers learn safety and skills. These cost a little, but parents and guardians of teens may be willing to pay for these courses. Driving schools exist, but avoid scams by doing your research on line. Some are not approved in your state, therefore will not help reduce car insurance rates. Do your research! I do not recommend anyone, or take money for mentioning online courses.

Students need hours and hours of practice. Some states require 40 hours plus 10 hours at night, just to get a provisional license! Sometimes, also 6 hours of driving with a licensed driving instructor!

Adults who are licensed but not very experienced could be helped by driving instructors, to make them safer. Many adults have developed some bad habits, like turning their head to talk to a passenger, while driving. This is very common, and can lead to disaster! Another habit to erase is not using turn signals! This happens extremely frequently.

Motorcycles can unnerve drivers, because they sometimes drive faster than cars, and sometimes pass cars in between lanes! Once you learn how to judge your position in a lane, you can become polite to a driver on a motorcycle, and let them through safely by a slight adjustment in your lane. Many will wave a thank-you to you for helping keep them safe! At the same time, you become safer by helping avoid a disaster.

Bicyclists can unnerve drivers, if they ride side by side. They should only ride in a straight line, but many do not. Plan ahead, and you may not kill a rider, or seriously injure them. An accident like that could really ruin your day. Look ahead for riders, and find your safety zone, which is room to move aside if the road is wide enough with light traffic. Otherwise, you may have to slow down temporarily.

Pedestrians have the right-of-way on city streets. Only a few cities have flashing lights to warn you of people crossing in crosswalks.

Stop signs are different from stop lights. Pedestrians can walk in a crosswalk after a vehicle comes to a stop. They may not cross the street if a stop light shows green for vehicles. They should only cross when the direction they are crossing has a green light. A few cities have electric signs showing "Walk" or "Stop" at intersections. These are usually only on busy streets. Stay focused so you are not distracted, and you should not need to worry about hurting a pedestrian, or getting a ticket.

CHAPTER FIVE
Avoid Distractions!!

CHAPTER FIVE

AVOID DISTRACTIONS!! As mentioned in Chapter 3, Distractions are causing most accidents!! Teens are more active between Memorial Day and Labor Day in America, (when school is less busy) so more distracted driving is occurring then, causing more accidents than normal.

Distractions for teens include looking away from the road to talk to a friend in the car, texting, or calling on the phone or answering the phone. I have experienced many adults doing the same thing. For example, when a car is slow to move forward in traffic, many times the driver can be seen looking down at their phone! (Don't look at other drivers because it is a distraction.) In traffic, you wouldn't believe drivers put on make-up, look for objects on other seats in the car, read maps, and read texts, all while moving slowly ahead. Many rear end collisions are caused by this.

Other distractions are sightseeing, in a new area, looking for friends on the sidewalks, especially around schools, and scenery which catches your eye. Billboards and signs should only be glanced at, not stared at. Even road warnings should be seen by quick reads of one or two words at a time! Get eyes back on the road, and your mirrors, as quickly as possible.

Distractions increase with the number of passengers in the car.

The driver has trouble using the skills of driving. It only takes a second to be distracted. Laughter and music in the background can distract any driver, at any age. Many things can go wrong: Eating while driving;

Putting on make-up; Changing stations on the radio; Sneezing!

Text messaging has become the largest culprit in car accidents!

Sending, obviously, makes no sense while moving in a car. Receiving is also a poor choice. Responding can wait!! It won't matter if a few minutes go by before you, the driver, can pull over on a street, or can exit a freeway, and stop somewhere where it is safe to respond. Very few texts are emergencies!!

Very few phone calls are emergencies!! Please make good decisions about phone calls. You can let a passenger take a call. You can let the caller leave a message. It is better to be alive or at least conscious, than dead because of a poor decision regarding a phone call.

The odds of a car crash are FOUR times greater when using a cell phone!

This book is only information. How you use this information is up to you.

Your conduct on the road can be affected by many things going on in your mind. Please concentrate just on driving while you are behind the wheel, for your own sake!

CHAPTER SIX

Prepare & Plan Ahead!

CHAPTER SIX

PREPARE & PLAN AHEAD! Three things should be kept in any car: Registration, Proof of Insurance, & a First Aid Kit.

Keep your windshield clean! A rag, and a squeegee, plus glass cleaner will take care of it. Vision is critical for driving a car.

Check your oil level weekly, until you determine your car is not leaking oil. Change your oil when the manufacturer suggests. 5,000 mile intervals may not be right for all vehicles. Read the manual for your car, or call a dealer.

Check your tire pressure. Learn how to do this, by asking a parent or friend. Tires differ in the number of pounds of pressure that is recommended. Don't over inflate tires, because driving increases the temperature in the tire, and can damage the tire. Your tires should also have a minimum of 1/16 inch of tread depth. Ask a tire dealer about the Lincoln head penny trick!

Do not procrastinate on recommended maintenance. Just like oil, coolant (radiator water plus chemicals,) transmission fluid, and brake fluids should be checked monthly, or when an engine light comes on your dashboard. Overheated engines will fail quickly, and may be expensive to fix.

When you go to a mechanic, be sure they are qualified to do the work. Ask if they use OEM (Original Equipment Manufacturer) quality parts. High-tech vehicles are too difficult to service by the owner. Computers are found throughout newer cars!

Air filters are important parts of a car, and need to be changed regularly, for your health, and for the health of your car!

Learn to put loose bags and suitcases in the trunk of the car. You do not want to get hit by one during an accident.

Adjust your rear-view mirror, and the two side mirrors before you drive. Also adjust your seat, if someone else has driven the car you are in now. Most people never adjust their head rests on the top of their seat. Put them at the center of the back of the head, and as close to the head as possible, ideally three inches behind. This could prevent serious spinal or neck injuries. Seat belts have a shoulder harness that will help with forward moving crashes.

CHAPTER SEVEN
Parking Lots

CHAPTER SEVEN

PARKING LOTS! Parking lots can be nightmares for non-experienced drivers. First Rule: Move Slowly, especially when you are backing out of a parking place. Check your surroundings before you enter or back out of a space. Check your surroundings before you return to your car. Check your surroundings after you sit down, buckle up, and start the car. I know, that was 4 rules.

There are many details about parking lots that take concentration to safely navigate your car.

Second Rule: As you enter a parking lot, make sure you can completely leave the road you were just on, by checking your rear view mirror, and checking for pedestrians ahead of you. You should have your turn signal on fifty to one hundred feet before you turn into the lot.

Once you are in the lot safely, Move Slowly, checking your surroundings for cross traffic, both cars and pedestrians. Continue moving slowly so you can see openings for parking. As much as you can, move down the aisles in the middle!! This allows you to avoid cars backing out, and cars coming toward you, if the isle is narrow. You may have to back up to avoid a car. Be ready!

Third Rule: PRACTICE moving into a parking space. Some are wide, but some are narrow. In the beginning stages of PRACTICE, go to a deserted or partially empty parking lot. Spend several minutes each time turning right into a space, then

Caring Mike

backing out, then go to another and turn left into a space. Don't practice backing into spaces until you are much more experienced.

Fourth Rule: Check your surroundings when you are backing out of, or pulling into a parking space. Do more than use your three mirrors (and a backup camera when reversing.) You must also look over your right shoulder through the back passenger window. Then look over your left shoulder through the back passenger window. Then finally, look through the back window for brake lights or white reverse lights on cars behind you. Edge back slowly with your foot off the gas when backing. Of course, have your foot on the brake. Cars in the aisle have priority over you, called the right-of-way.

When pulling INTO a parking space, check to see if the driver or any passengers are opening their doors to exit their vehicle. (Many do this without looking!)

Again, look for pedestrians, many of whom are distracted by kids, groceries, texting, or talking on their cell phone. They may not see you! They may be hidden from your sight, so roll down your window to possibly hear them walking or talking, when weather permits this.

CHAPTER EIGHT
Practice

CHAPTER EIGHT

Let's review important parts of this book.

PRACTICE! PRACTICE! PRACTICE! Extremely important.

Remember that traffic fatalities are rising! The numbers were slowing in the years preceding 2016, but no longer!

Drivers are traveling more, but fatalities are now twice the percent of the percentage increase in traffic. You must take driving more seriously than years ago!

Establish good habits behind the wheel. This book is purposely not the length of a novel. Please read it over many times, at your convenience, until you can remember the important parts.

DO NOT Use A Cell Phone while behind the wheel. This is so logical, when you think about it.

Learn to be comfortable with lane changes. Use your mirrors by making quick glances and quick head turns to check the blind spots.

Always look ahead in between these quick checks!

If you must drive for several hours, be sure to schedule a stop to recharge. This could be a short walk, and/or getting some caffeine beverage if you didn't get enough sleep the night before.

STAY SAFE!! STAY ALIVE!!

Caring Mike Publishing LLC assumes no responsibility for any driver error, any accident, any damage, injury, or death due to driving, or being a passenger inside a vehicle, nor as a pedestrian.

This also includes rare medical, mental, or physical occurrences to any driver or pedestrian involved in a collision, including heart attack, stroke, blindness, or vehicle failure.

Printed in Great Britain
by Amazon